OUR PERSONAL AFFAIRS PORTFOLIO

Important Information About Our
Life, Estate, and Wishes

....

NAME & DATE

....

NAME & DATE

CONFIDENTIAL

This portfolio contains confidential information
and should be stored in a safe place.

Published by 55 Plus ES, LLC
www.55PlusES.com
Copyright © 2023 Susan Loumagne

Author: Susan Loumagne

Graphic Support: Lawrence Phillips

ISBN: 979-8-9867618-0-0 (paperback)
ISBN: 979-8-9867618-2-4 (hardcover)

This book is not a legal document nor is it a Will.
No liability is assumed for losses or damages due to the information provided.

TABLE OF CONTENTS

Useful listings for replacements of important documents, government resources, and support organizations

Use these pages to list the "to-dos" to assist in completing your portfolio

PART 1

You'll combine your information in the following seven sections

Name, parents' names, children, employment, volunteerism, military service, and storage of important papers

Include contacts who are important to you.

Name, type of pet, veterinarian, medications, vaccines, microchip status, pet insurance, notable markings, health conditions, and your pet care service

Banking, credit cards, personal income, financial advisor and investments,
insurance policies – life, property, auto, health, dental, and storage of taxes

Real estate – home, investment, and vacation, vehicles, loans given, stored
hidden assets, lockbox/safe deposit box, and personal property

Record your obligations for household bills and recurring payments

Record purchases, model and serial numbers, purchase date, and any other
useful information

Parts 2 and 3 are duplicates, with 10 sections for each person.

Use this section to record information about a business, partnership,
investments, or anything else you haven't shared in any other section.

Company or site, username, and password to access

Doctors, medical conditions, medical equipment, vision, allergies,
and vaccines and immunizations

THE PERSONAL AFFAIRS PORTFOLIO

Welcome ~

Here are some recommendations for completing your Portfolio

✓ *Review the Table of Contents to familiarize yourself with the Portfolio's layout and organization for couples*

✓ *Read the Quick Start Guide, which provides helpful tips and guidance for completing your Portfolio.*

✓ *Only complete the sections that are relevant to you.*

✓ *Use the To Do Notes pages to keep track of tasks you need to do, items you need to find, or important documents you need to replace.*

✓ *Take the time to discuss your wishes and designations with your loved ones or your attorney. Let them know where you are storing your Portfolio for easy access.*

✓ *Remember to review and update your Portfolio yearly to keep it current and reflective of any changes in your life.*

✓ *If you've found this planner useful, please leave a review on Amazon.*

Addtinal versions of this Portfolio are available on Amazon.com

MY PERSONAL AFFAIRS PORTFOLIO - comprehensive and for singles or couples

JUST THE FACTS - short, concise, and for singles

OUR JUST THE FACTS - short, concise, and for couples

DIGITAL - available by emailing Info@55pluses.com

This planner is not a legal document.

QUICK START GUIDE

How quickly you complete this Portfolio is up to you, and remember, you do not need to fill in every field on your forms. The following tips will help ensure that you complete your Portfolio.

1: Schedule It!

Block off time this week to begin working on your Portfolio. At the end of the session, schedule the next time you will work on completing the next sections.

2: Do it!

You may want to work with a partner. One person writes while the other dictates the information. Only fill in the information you feel comfortable adding. For example, you may want to use only the last 4 digits of your Social Security number or credit card account.

3: Keep a To-Do List!

Use these pages to keep a master list of what information and documents you need to find, copy, or replace.

4: Photograph and Video It!

Take photos of your family, pets, the contents of your house, the exterior, and anything else you want to have a visual record. Videos and photos can be helpful for identification, insurance claims and creating your will.

5: Follow Up!

Order copies of missing documents and complete all lingering tasks on your list. The Resource Pages have links to help you obtain originals of any essential missing cards or documents.

6: Store It!

We recommend storing this Portfolio with your essential legal and estate documents, photos, letters to loved ones, and other necessary and important items you've referenced. It's wise to purchase a fireproof and waterproof lockbox with a one-hour (minimum) fireproof rating to store these items.

7: Share It!

Let trusted people know that you have this Portfolio and where it is stored. It may also be the perfect time to initiate hard-to-have conversations to discuss your estate and let people know your wishes.

WHAT YOU NEED TO GATHER FOR EACH SECTION

Personal Profile

Gather the following list of items. We recommend making copies and storing them in a waterproof and fireproof lockbox.

- ✓ Driver's License
- ✓ Social Security Card
- ✓ Medicare Card
- ✓ Passport
- ✓ Adoption Records
- ✓ Marriage License
- ✓ Divorce Record
- ✓ Death Certificates
- ✓ Children's contact information

Important Contacts

Include key contacts you or your family may want to have handy. For example, include family, friends, neighbors, handypersons, your place of employment, volunteer communities, and anyone else important to you. In addition, you can list your service providers, such as internet, electric company, etc., here or in the monthly bill section.

- ✓ Address book and cell phone for important contacts' phone numbers and addresses

Pets

Having information about your pets at hand is so valuable. We've included pages for two pets, so contact us if you need additional pages.   info@55pluses.com

- ✓ Veterinarian's name and number
- ✓ Medications and vaccines
- ✓ Health records
- ✓ Pet sitter and dog walker

Finances

Keeping your financial information together in one place is of paramount importance. Our lives revolve around our finances, so having your information organized brings true peace of mind. Now is an excellent time to review current insurance policies to see if you have the coverage you need. If you rent a house or apartment, consider getting an affordable renters insurance policy to cover the contents of your home.

- ✓ Bank account numbers
- ✓ Credit cards - company details, and if you want the last 4 numbers on the cards
- ✓ Financial services companies
- ✓ Investments
- ✓ Outstanding loans
- ✓ Retirement income information
- ✓ Insurance policies
- ✓ Health insurance card
- ✓ Prescription card

Assets

What do you own? This section will help you sort it out and keep it all together. This is well worth the effort because this information is a valuable tool that can assist when planning for retirement, writing your Will, making an insurance claim, or making life a bit easier for others.

- ✓ Real Estate - property addresses, ownership deeds, and mortgage contracts
- ✓ Vehicle owner's cards
- ✓ Loans given or notes
- ✓ Personal Property that has monetary value, such as jewelry, coins, gun collection, and property with sentimental/heirloom value

You will be recording information about your:

- ✓ Will
- ✓ Advance Medical Directive
- ✓ Healthcare Power of Attorney
- ✓ Financial Durable Power of Attorney

Monthly Bills, Subscriptions, and Giving

Think of all the payments you make throughout the year. What if someone needed to manage these payments on your behalf? Completing this section gives someone a complete picture of what needs to be paid and how it's paid. Reviewing all your subscriptions is helpful, so you are not paying for something you no longer want or use.

- ✓ Include publications, memberships, subscriptions, and giving
- ✓ Bills/Invoices, whether they occur monthly, quarterly, semiannually, or annually

Household Inventory

This section is an excellent place to consolidate information about your large purchases for insurance or warranty purposes, so consider taking photos or videos.

- ✓ Item description and location
- ✓ Purchased where and when
- ✓ Original and replacement cost
- ✓ Model number/Serial number

PARTS 2 and 3

Additional Information

Use this section to record information about a business, partnership, investments, or anything else you haven't shared in any other section.

Passwords

Keeping track of a multitude of passwords can be a challenge. After entering the information, print the list and keep it handy to use, but keep it confidential.

You will need to gather the following

- ✓ Company, username and passwords
- ✓ Add social media passwords

Medical Information

Record your most pertinent medical information regarding your doctors, vaccines, and any health conditions.

- ✓ Doctors' names and specialties
- ✓ Dates of Vaccines – shingles, pneumonia, covid, and others

Medications

The Medications Form is an excellent way to keep track of all the medications you take, and why you take them. You should also record your over-the-counter (OTC) medications and vitamins. Each person can fill out a Medication's To Go Form at the end of Part One and Part Two. Cut it out of this book and keep it with you to show medical personnel.

- ✓ All prescribed medications
- ✓ All over-the-counter medicines and vitamins

Estate and Legal Documents

In this section, you'll record the details of your must-have legal documents. Everyone needs a Will, so take the time to do it now so the courts aren't making the decisions about your estate. Creating these documents with a lawyer is a wise choice, or you may use an online service. It's helpful to discuss the documents with the persons to whom you have chosen as your executor and assigned power of attorney.

If I Can't Talk or I'm Incapacitated

Write instructions on what needs to be taken care of, who to contact, and anything else you would like to say if you are unable to communicate.

Final Wishes

Take this opportunity to share your preferences for your final wishes. Any insights you provide will be a gift to whoever plans your funeral.

. You'll record information about:

- ✓ Any pre-planning documentation
- ✓ Church, clergy, and cemetery information
- ✓ Your choice of final disposition
- ✓ Your preferences for your service, graveside, and reception

Thoughts, Words, and Wishes

Take the opportunity to share your thoughts. What motivates you in life, the words you live by, and any wishes for the future.

Letters to Loved Ones

Take this opportunity to write a letter or thoughts to a loved one. You can leave the letter in this book or, for privacy, take out the page and put the letter in an envelope. You can put the envelope back in the book or store with your other important documents.

RESOURCES

Vital Records

Birth, Death, Marriage, and Divorce Records   www.cdc.gov/nchs/w2w.htm
Links to your state's Bureau of Vital Statistics

Government Programs

Medicare   www.medicare.gov
800-633-4227

Social Security Office   www.socialsecurity.gov
800-772-1213

Veterans Administration   www.va.gov
800-827-1000

Veterans Service Records National Archives   www.archives.gov/veterans
866-272-6272

U.S. Passports   www.travel.state.gov
877-487-2778

Estate and Must Have Documents

Wills, Healthcare Directives, and Durable Power of Attorney

National Academy of Elder Law Attorneys   www.naela.org
703-942-5711

Legal Zoom   www.legalzoom.com
800-773-0888

Emergency Preparation & Disaster Relief

American Red Cross   www.redcross.org
800-733-2767

FEMA – Federal Emergency Management Association www.fema.gov
800-621-3362

Ready.gov   www.ready.gov
800-621-3362

Centers for Disease Control and Prevention   www.cdc.gov
800-232-4636

Support Organizations

Cancer Support Community   www.cancersupportcommunity.org
202-659-9709

American Heart Association   www.heart.org
800-242-8721

American Cancer Society   www.cancer.org
800-227-2345

American Diabetes Association   www.diabetes.org
800-342-2383

Alzheimer's Association   www.alz.org
800-272-3900 (24/7 Helpline)

American Lung Association   www.lung.org
800-586-4872

Operation Hope   www.operationhope.org
213-891-2900

The Salvation Army   www.salvationarmyusa.org
800-SAL-ARMY

Pets

The Humane Society   www.humanesociety.org
866-720-2676

Caregiving & Eldercare Assistance

National Caregivers Library   www.caregiverslibrary.org
804-327-1111

Eldercare   www.eldercare.gov
800-677-1116

National Association of Professional Care Managers   www.caremanager.org
520-881-8008

Companion Items for your Personal Affairs Portfolio

The Personal Affairs Portfolio   www.55PlusES.com

TO DO NOTES

....
....
....
....
....
....
....
....
....
....
....
....
....
....
....
....
....
....
....
....
....

TO DO NOTES

....
....
....
....
....
....
....
....
....
....
....
....
....
....
....
....
....
....
....
....
....
....
....
....

PERSONAL PROFILE - PERSON 1

Name: ....Nationality: ....

Birth Date: .... Place of Birth: ....

Name on Birth Certificate: ....

Mother's Maiden Name: ....Living? ....

....

Father's Name: .... Living? ....

....

Relationship Status: .... Spouse/Partner's Name: ....

....

Employer: ....

Job and Title: ....

Supervisor's Name and Phone Number: ....

....

Volunteer Organizations and Contact: ....

....

....

Military Branch: .... Rank: ....

Dates Served and Where? ....

NOTES: ....

....

....

....

....

IMPORTANT PAPERS

Examples of important papers are social security card, birth certificate, passport, driver's license, military DD214, marriage license, divorce record, resident alien card, adoption record, frequent traveler #

Type	Number	Stored Where?	Copy Y/N

PERSONAL PROFILE - PERSON 2

Name: ....Nationality: ....

Birth Date: .... Place of Birth: ....

Name on Birth Certificate: ....

Mother's Maiden Name: ....Living? ....

....

Father's Name: .... Living? ....

....

Relationship Status: .... Spouse/Partner's Name: ....

....

Employer: ....

Job and Title: ....

Supervisor's Name and Phone Number: ....

....

Volunteer Organizations and Contact: ....

....

....

Military Branch: .... Rank: ....

Dates Served and Where? ....

_____

NOTES: ....

....

....

....

....

IMPORTANT PAPERS

Examples of important papers are social security card, birth certificate, passport, driver's license, military DD214, marriage license, divorce record, resident alien card, adoption record, frequent traveler #

Type	Number	Stored Where?	Copy Y/N

CHILDREN

Name of Parents: ....

Given Name: ....

Date of Birth: .... Place of Birth: ....

SS#: .... Phone Number: ....

Address: ....

Given Name: ....

Date of Birth: .... Place of Birth: ....

SS#: .... Phone Number: ....

Address: ....

Given Name: ....

Date of Birth: .... Place of Birth: ....

SS#: .... Phone Number: ....

Address: ....

Given Name: ....

Date of Birth: .... Place of Birth: ....

SS#: .... Phone Number: ....

Address: ....

Given Name: ....

Date of Birth: .... Place of Birth: ....

SS#: .... Phone Number: ....

Address: ....

CHILDREN

Name of Parents: ....

Given Name: ....

Date of Birth: .... Place of Birth: ....

SS#: .... Phone Number: ....

Address: ....

_____

Given Name: ....

Date of Birth: .... Place of Birth: ....

SS#: .... Phone Number: ....

Address: ....

_____

Given Name: ....

Date of Birth: .... Place of Birth: ....

SS#: .... Phone Number: ....

Address: ....

_____

Given Name: ....

Date of Birth: .... Place of Birth: ....

SS#: .... Phone Number: ....

Address: ....

_____

Given Name: ....

Date of Birth: .... Place of Birth: ....

SS#: .... Phone Number: ....

Address: ....

SIBLINGS - Person 1

Name .... Living?: ....

Date of Birth: .... Phone: ....

Email or Address: ....

Name .... Living?: ....

Date of Birth: .... Phone: ....

Email or Address: ....

Name .... Living?: ....

Date of Birth: .... Phone: ....

Email or Address: ....

Name .... Living?: ....

Date of Birth: .... Phone: ....

Email or Address: ....

Name .... Living?: ....

Date of Birth: .... Phone: ....

Email or Address: ....

Name .... Living?: ....

Date of Birth .... Phone: ....

Email or Address: ....

SIBLINGS - Person 2

Name.. Living?:.............................

Date of Birth: .... Phone: ....

Email or Address: ....

_____

Name.. Living?:.............................

Date of Birth: .... Phone: ....

Email or Address: ....

_____

Name.. Living?:.............................

Date of Birth: .... Phone: ....

Email or Address: ....

_____

Name.. Living?:.............................

Date of Birth: .... Phone: ....

Email or Address: ....

_____

Name.. Living?:.............................

Date of Birth: .... Phone: ....

Email or Address: ....

_____

Name.. Living?:.............................

Date of Birth: .... Phone: ....

Email or Address: ....

PAST MARRIAGES

Your Name: ....

Name of Former Spouse: ....

Date of Marriage .... Place of Marriage ....

Marriage ended by: .... Copy of Marriage License: ....

Date and Place of Divorce: ....

Copy of Divorce Papers: .... Copy of Death Certificate: ....

Email or Phone Number (if living): ....

Your Name: ....

Name of Former Spouse: ....

Date of Marriage .... Place of Marriage ....

Marriage ended by: .... Copy of Marriage License: ....

Date and Place of Divorce: ....

Copy of Divorce Papers: .... Copy of Death Certificate: ....

Email or Phone Number (if living): ....

Your Name: ....

Name of Former Spouse: ....

Date of Marriage .... Place of Marriage ....

Marriage ended by: .... Copy of Marriage License: ....

Date and Place of Divorce: ....

Copy of Divorce Papers: .... Copy of Death Certificate: ....

Email or Phone Number (if living): ....

IMPORTANT CONTACTS

Name: .... Relationship: ....

Phone:... Email: ....

Address: ....

Name: .... Relationship: ....

Phone:... Email: ....

Address: ....

Name: .... Relationship: ....

Phone:... Email: ....

Address: ....

Name: .... Relationship: ....

Phone:... Email: ....

Address: ....

Name: .... Relationship: ....

Phone:... Email: ....

Address: ....

Name: .... Relationship: ....

Phone:... Email: ....

Address: ....

IMPORTANT CONTACTS

Name: .... Relationship: ....

Phone:.. Email: ....

Address: ....

Name: .... Relationship: ....

Phone:.. Email: ....

Address: ....

Name: .... Relationship: ....

Phone:.. Email: ....

Address: ....

Name: .... Relationship: ....

Phone:.. Email: ....

Address: ....

Name: .... Relationship: ....

Phone:.. Email: ....

Address: ....

Name: .... Relationship: ....

Phone:.. Email: ....

Address: ....

IMPORTANT CONTACTS

Name: .... Relationship: ....

Phone:.. Email: ....

Address: ....

Name: .... Relationship: ....

Phone:.. Email: ....

Address: ....

Name: .... Relationship: ....

Phone:.. Email: ....

Address: ....

Name: .... Relationship: ....

Phone:.. Email: ....

Address: ....

Name: .... Relationship: ....

Phone:.. Email: ....

Address: ....

Name: .... Relationship: ....

Phone:.. Email: ....

Address: ....

PET INFORMATION - 1

Pet Name: .... Date of Birth: .... Age: ....

Breed: .... Coat Color: ....

☐ Canine/Dog ☐ Feline/Cat ☐ Other .... ☐ Neutered or Spayed

Notable markings on pet: ....

Veterinarian name and phone number: ....

....

24-hour Veterinarian name and phone number: ....

....

Is this a service animal with certification? ....

Where do you keep the certification document? ....

Any Medical or Behavioral Alerts? Seizures, caution with humans or other animals, adverse reactions to medications, allergies, blind, or deaf.

....

....

IDENTIFICATION

Does your pet have identification tags with your name and phone number? Y ☐ N ☐

What name and number are on the tags? ....

....

Does your pet have a microchip or tattoo? ....

....

What is the number? ....

....

Local shelter name and phone number: ....

....

Local shelter name and phone number: ....

....

VACCINES

Common Vaccines: Bordetella, Lepto, DHPP, DHLPP, Rattlesnake, FVRCP, Feline Leukemia

Where do you keep the vaccine records? ....

Date of last Rabies vaccine: ....

Name of Vaccine: .... Date: ....

Name of Vaccine: .... Date: ....

Name of Vaccine: .... Date: ....

Name of Vaccine: .... Date: ....

Name of Vaccine: .... Date: ....

Name of Vaccine: .... Date: ....

MEDICATIONS

Is your pet on medications? ....

Name of medications: ....

....

Where do you purchase medications? ....

....

If online, what is the website and account information?...

....

Account User ID: .... Password: ....

Are your orders on auto-delivery? ....

....

Additional notes: ....

....

INSURANCE

Do you have pet insurance? ....

....

What is the company name and policy number? ....

....

....

PET CARE SERVICE

List the people or companies you use for walking, feeding, or overnights.

Name: ....Phone Number: ....

Name: ....Phone Number: ....

LONG-TERM CARE PLANNING

Have you designated someone to care for your pet if you are unable? ....

Name and contact information: ....

....

Details of the arrangement: ....

....

....

....

Have you done estate planning for your pet and included it as part of your Will? ....

Details of the arrangement: ....

....

....

....

Additional notes about your pet: ....

....

PET INFORMATION - 2

Pet Name: .... Date of Birth: .... Age: ....

Breed: .... Coat Color: ....

☐ Canine/Dog ☐ Feline/Cat ☐ Other .... ☐ Neutered or Spayed

Notable markings on pet: ....

Veterinarian name and phone number: ....

....

24-hour Veterinarian name and phone number: ....

....

Is this a service animal with certification? ....

Where do you keep the certification document? ....

Any Medical or Behavioral Alerts? Seizures, caution with humans or other animals, adverse reactions to medications, allergies, blind, or deaf.

....

....

IDENTIFICATION

Does your pet have identification tags with your name and phone number? Y ☐ N ☐

What name and number are on the tags? ....

....

Does your pet have a microchip or tattoo? ....

....

What is the number? ....

....

Local shelter name and phone number: ....

....

Local shelter name and phone number: ....

....

VACCINES

Common Vaccines: Bordetella, Lepto, DHPP, DHLPP, Rattlesnake, FVRCP, Feline Leukemia

Where do you keep the vaccine records? ....

Date of last rabies vaccine: ....

Name of Vaccine: .... Date: ....

Name of Vaccine: .... Date: ....

Name of Vaccine: .... Date: ....

Name of Vaccine: .... Date: ....

Name of Vaccine: .... Date: ....

Name of Vaccine: .... Date: ....

MEDICATIONS

Is your pet on medications? ....

Name of medications: ....

....

Where do you purchase medications? ....

....

If online, what is the website and account information?...

....

Account User ID: .... Password: ....

Are your orders on auto-delivery? ....

....

Additional notes: ....

....

INSURANCE

Do you have pet insurance? ....

....

What is the company name and policy number? ....

....

....

PET CARE SERVICE

List the name of the people or companies you use for walking, feeding, or overnights.

Name: .... Phone Number: ....

Name: .... Phone Number: ....

LONG-TERM CARE PLANNING

Have you designated someone to care for your pet if you are unable? ....

Name and contact information: ....

....

Details of the arrangement: ....

....

....

....

Have you done estate planning for your pet and included it as part of your Will? ....

Details of the arrangement: ....

....

....

....

Additional notes about your pet: ....

....

FINANCES

BANKING   *Add log-in information to Password page.*

Name of Bank: ....

Branch Location: ....

Contact's Name: .... Phone No: ....

Account Type	Account Number * optional	Name on Account

Notes: ....

Name of Bank: ....

Branch Location: ....

Contact's Name: .... Phone No: ....

Account Type	Account Number * optional	Name on Account

Notes: ....

Name of Bank: ....

Branch Location: ....

Contact's Name: .... Phone No: ....

Account Type	Account Number * optional	Name on Account

Notes: ....

CREDIT CARDS

* Account number and security code optional.   *Add log-in information to the Passwords page.*

Name of Company: .... Phone No: ....

Name on Account: ....

Account Number: .... Security Code: ....

Expiration: .... Balance Insured: ....

Name of Company: .... Phone No: ....

Name on Account: ....

Account Number: .... Security Code: ....

Expiration: .... Balance Insured: ....

Name of Company: .... Phone No: ....

Name on Account: ....

Account Number: .... Security Code: ....

Expiration: .... Balance Insured: ....

Name of Company: .... Phone No: ....

Name on Account: ....

Account Number: .... Security Code: ....

Expiration: .... Balance Insured: ....

Name of Company: .... Phone No: ....

Name on Account: ....

Account Number: .... Security Code: ....

Expiration: .... Balance Insured: ....

CREDIT CARDS

Name of Company: .... Phone No: ....

Name on Account: ....

Account Number: .... Security Code: ....

Expiration: .... Balance Insured: ....

Name of Company: .... Phone No: ....

Name on Account: ....

Account Number: .... Security Code: ....

Expiration: .... Balance Insured: ....

Name of Company: .... Phone No: ....

Name on Account: ....

Account Number: .... Security Code: ....

Expiration: .... Balance Insured: ....

Name of Company: .... Phone No: ....

Name on Account: ....

Account Number: .... Security Code: ....

Expiration: .... Balance Insured: ....

Name of Company: .... Phone No: ....

Name on Account: ....

Account Number: .... Security Code: ....

Expiration: .... Balance Insured: ....

FINANCIAL SERVICES

Company Name: ....

Advisor's Name: .... Phone Number: ....

Email: ....

Notes: ....

....

Company Name: ....

Advisor's Name: .... Phone Number: ....

Email: ....

Notes: ....

....

Company Name: ....

Advisor's Name: .... Phone Number: ....

Email: ....

Notes: ....

....

CERTIFICATE OF DEPOSIT

Bank: ....

Amount: .... Interest Rate: .... Maturity Date: ....

Bank: ....

Amount: .... Interest Rate: .... Maturity Date: ....

Note about additional CD's: ....

....

SAVINGS BONDS

Where are they stored? ....

....

INVESTMENTS

Name: ....

Investment Type: ....   * 401K, IRA, Mutual Funds, Stocks, Bitcoin, NFTs

Held By: .... Phone Number: ....

Account Number: ....

Notes: ....

....

Investment Type: ....   * 401K, IRA, Mutual Funds, Stocks, Bitcoin, NFTs

Held By: .... Phone Number: ....

Account Number: ....

Notes: ....

....

Investment Type: ....   * 401K, IRA, Mutual Funds, Stocks, Bitcoin, NFTs

Held By: .... Phone Number: ....

Account Number: ....

Notes: ....

....

Investment Type: ....   * 401K, IRA, Mutual Funds, Stocks, Bitcoin, NFTs

Held By: .... Phone Number: ....

Account Number: ....

Notes: ....

....

Investment Type: ....   * 401K, IRA, Mutual Funds, Stocks, Bitcoin, NFTs

Held By: .... Phone Number: ....

Account Number: ....

Notes: ....

....

INVESTMENTS

Name: ....

Investment Type: ....   * 401K, IRA, Mutual Funds, Stocks, Bitcoin, NFTs

Held By: .... Phone Number: ....

Account Number: ....

Notes: ....

....

Investment Type: ....   * 401K, IRA, Mutual Funds, Stocks, Bitcoin, NFTs

Held By: .... Phone Number: ....

Account Number: ....

Notes: ....

....

Investment Type: ....   * 401K, IRA, Mutual Funds, Stocks, Bitcoin, NFTs

Held By: .... Phone Number: ....

Account Number: ....

Notes: ....

....

Investment Type: ....   * 401K, IRA, Mutual Funds, Stocks, Bitcoin, NFTs

Held By: .... Phone Number: ....

Account Number: ....

Notes: ....

....

Investment Type: ....   * 401K, IRA, Mutual Funds, Stocks, Bitcoin, NFTs

Held By: .... Phone Number: ....

Account Number: ....

Notes: ....

....

PERSONAL INCOME

This section covers any income you receive; salary, social security, pensions, annuities, military, trusts, royalties, bonuses, dividends, interest, alimony, or any other income.

Type:* ....

Company: .... Phone: ....

Amount: .... Note: ....

_____

Type:* ....

Company: .... Phone: ....

Amount: .... Note: ....

_____

Type:* ....

Company: .... Phone: ....

Amount: .... Note: ....

_____

Type:* ....

Company: .... Phone: ....

Amount: .... Note: ....

_____

Type:* ....

Company: .... Phone: ....

Amount: .... Note: ....

_____

Type:* ....

Company: .... Phone: ....

Amount: .... Note: ....

_____

Type:* ....

Company: .... Phone: ....

Amount: .... Note: ....

PERSONAL INCOME

This section covers any income you receive; salary, social security, pensions, annuities, military, trusts, royalties, bonuses, dividends, interest, alimony, or any other income.

Type:* ....

Company: .... Phone: ....

Amount: .... Note: ....

Type:* ....

Company: .... Phone: ....

Amount: .... Note: ....

Type:* ....

Company: .... Phone: ....

Amount: .... Note: ....

Type:* ....

Company: .... Phone: ....

Amount: .... Note: ....

Type:* ....

Company: .... Phone: ....

Amount: .... Note: ....

Type:* ....

Company: .... Phone: ....

Amount: .... Note: ....

Type:* ....

Company: .... Phone: ....

Amount: .... Note: ....

AUTO INSURANCE

Vehicle, make, model, Vin# is also in the Assets section.

Company: .... Phone: ....

Policy Number: .... Where is policy? ....

Agent Name: .... Agent phone: ....

Company: .... Phone: ....

Policy Number: .... Where is policy? ....

Agent Name: .... Agent phone: ....

HEALTH, DENTAL, AND PRESCRIPTION INSURANCE

Name on Policy: ....

Company: .... Phone: ....

Policy Number: .... Where is policy? ....

Coverage: ....

Notes: ....

....

Name on Policy: ....

Company: .... Phone: ....

Policy Number: .... Where is policy? ....

Coverage: ....

Notes: ....

....

Name on Policy: ....

Company: .... Phone: ....

Policy Number: .... Where is policy? ....

Coverage: ....

Notes: ....

....

AUTO INSURANCE

Vehicle, make, model, Vin# is also in the Assets section.

Company: .... Phone: ....

Policy Number: .... Where is policy? ....

Agent Name: .... Agent phone: ....

Company: .... Phone: ....

Policy Number: .... Where is policy? ....

Agent Name: .... Agent phone: ....

HEALTH, DENTAL, AND PRESCRIPTION INSURANCE

Name on Policy: ....

Company: .... Phone: ....

Policy Number: .... Where is policy? ....

Coverage: ....

Notes: ....

....

Name on Policy: ....

Company: .... Phone: ....

Policy Number: .... Where is policy? ....

Coverage: ....

Notes: ....

....

Name on Policy: ....

Company: .... Phone: ....

Policy Number: .... Where is policy? ....

Coverage: ....

Notes: ....

....

LIFE INSURANCE

Name on Policy: ....

Company: .... Phone Number: ....

Agent: .... Phone Number: ....

Policy Number: .... Policy Stored Where? ....

Amount: .... Whole Life or Term: .... Length of Policy: ....

Notes: ....

Beneficiary Name: .... Phone Number: ....

Beneficiary Address: .... Aware of Designation? ....

Contingent Name: .... Phone Number: ....

_____

Name on Policy: ....

Company: .... Phone Number: ....

Agent: .... Phone Number: ....

Policy Number: .... Policy Stored Where? ....

Amount: .... Whole Life or Term: .... Length of Policy: ....

Notes: ....

Beneficiary Name: .... Phone Number: ....

Beneficiary Address: .... Aware of Designation? ....

Contingent Name: .... Phone Number: ....

_____

Do you have other employee/retiree sponsored supplemental life insurance plans?

Plan Name: ....

Details: ....

_____

Do you have other employee/retiree sponsored supplemental life insurance plans?

Plan Name: ....

Details: ....

....

....

LIFE INSURANCE

Name on Policy: ....

Company: .... Phone Number: ....

Agent: .... Phone Number: ....

Policy Number: .... Policy Stored Where? ....

Amount: .... Whole Life or Term: .... Length of Policy: ....

Notes: ....

Beneficiary Name: .... Phone Number: ....

Beneficiary Address: .... Aware of Designation? ....

Contingent Name: .... Phone Number: ....

_____

Name on Policy: ....

Company: .... Phone Number: ....

Agent: .... Phone Number: ....

Policy Number: .... Policy Stored Where? ....

Amount: .... Whole Life or Term: .... Length of Policy: ....

Notes: ....

Beneficiary Name: .... Phone Number: ....

Beneficiary Address: .... Aware of Designation? ....

Contingent Name: .... Phone Number: ....

_____

Do you have other employee/retiree sponsored supplemental life insurance plans?

Plan Name: ....

Details: ....

_____

Do you have other employee/retiree sponsored supplemental life insurance plans?

Plan Name: ....

Details: ....

....

....

ADDITIONAL INSURANCE

Type: ....

Company: .... Amount: ....

Policy Number: .... Stored? ....

Agent Name: .... Phone Number: ....

Notes: ....

Type: ....

Company: .... Amount: ....

Policy Number: .... Stored? ....

Agent Name: .... Phone Number: ....

Notes: ....

Type: ....

Company: .... Amount: ....

Policy Number: .... Stored? ....

Agent Name: .... Phone Number: ....

Notes: ....

Type: ....

Company: .... Amount: ....

Policy Number: .... Stored? ....

Agent Name: .... Phone Number: ....

Notes: ....

Type: ....

Company: .... Amount: ....

Policy Number: .... Stored? ....

Agent Name: .... Phone Number: ....

Notes: ....

LOANS YOU OWE

Loan From: .... Phone: ....

Account Number: ....

Type of Loan: .... Interest Rate: ....

Amount: .... Payment: ....

Date of Origination: .... Length of Loan: ....

Loan From: .... Phone: ....

Account Number: ....

Type of Loan: .... Interest Rate: ....

Amount: .... Payment: ....

Date of Origination: .... Length of Loan: ....

Loan From: .... Phone: ....

Account Number: ....

Type of Loan: .... Interest Rate: ....

Amount: .... Payment: ....

Date of Origination: .... Length of Loan: ....

Loan From: .... Phone: ....

Account Number: ....

Type of Loan: .... Interest Rate: ....

Amount: .... Payment: ....

Date of Origination: .... Length of Loan: ....

Loan From: .... Phone: ....

Account Number: ....

Type of Loan: .... Interest Rate: ....

Amount: .... Payment: ....

Date of Origination: .... Length of Loan: ....

INCOME TAX FILING

Where do you store previous years' tax returns? ....

Do you use a service to complete and file your taxes? ....

Online service information: ....

....

Accountant's name and email: ....

Notes: ....

ADDITIONAL FINANCIAL INFORMATION

Notes: ....

....

....

....

....

....

....

....

....

....

....

....

....

....

....

....

....

....

....

ASSETS

REAL ESTATE

Property Type: .... Home, Investment, Rental, Vacation

Address: ....

Purchase Date: .... Payment: ....

Mortgage Held By: ....

Balance of Loan: .... As of date: ....

Value of Property: .... As of date: ....

Homeowners Insurance Company: ....

Property Taxes - Amount and how are they paid?: ....

___

Property Type: .... Home, Investment, Rental, Vacation

Address: ....

Purchase Date: .... Payment: ....

Mortgage Held By: ....

Balance of Loan: .... As of date: ....

Value of Property: .... As of date: ....

Homeowners Insurance Company: ....

Property Taxes - Amount and how are they paid?: ....

___

Property Type: .... Home, Investment, Rental, Vacation

Address: ....

Purchase Date: .... Payment: ....

Mortgage Held By: ....

Balance of Loan: .... As of date: ....

Value of Property: .... As of date: ....

Homeowners Insurance Company: ....

Property Taxes - Amount and how are they paid?: ....

ASSETS

VEHICLES

Vehicle Type: .... * Automobile, Boat, Motorhome, Motorcycle, Truck, Van

Make: .... Model: .... Year: ....

Registered To: .... VIN#: ....

Status of Ownership: .... Title Stored? ....

Vehicle Type: .... * Automobile, Boat, Motorhome, Motorcycle, Truck, Van

Make: .... Model: .... Year: ....

Registered To: .... VIN#: ....

Status of Ownership: .... Title Stored? ....

Vehicle Type: .... * Automobile, Boat, Motorhome, Motorcycle, Truck, Van

Make: .... Model: .... Year: ....

Registered To: .... VIN#: ....

Status of Ownership: .... Title Stored? ....

Vehicle Type: .... * Automobile, Boat, Motorhome, Motorcycle, Truck, Van

Make: .... Model: .... Year: ....

Registered To: .... VIN#: ....

Status of Ownership: .... Title Stored? ....

Vehicle Type: .... * Automobile, Boat, Motorhome, Motorcycle, Truck, Van

Make: .... Model: .... Year: ....

Registered To: .... VIN#: ....

Status of Ownership: .... Title Stored? ....

STORAGE OF CODES, KEYS, AND PROPERTY

Garage Door Code .... Security System Code ....

Where do you keep extra keys for your house, cars, etc.? ....

....

....

Do you have a Storage Unit? Details: ....

....

....

DOCUMENTS AND VALUABLES STORAGE

Do you have a fireproof lockbox?   Where is it?   Where is the key or what is the code?

....

Do you have a safe deposit box?   Where is it?   Where is the key or what is the code?

....

STORED ASSETS

Many people store money or other valuables in secret locations, only to have their assets lost forever if they pass away without telling someone. If you have hidden assets or a storage unit, include that information here. Or, write the details down and store it in your safety deposit box or lockbox. Protect your assets.

Do you have assets hidden in your home?   Y ☐ N ☐

Does anyone else know the location? If yes, who? ....

If no one else knows, you should share the location or an obvious hint.

Location or hint? ....

....

Do you have assets stored in another location?   Y ☐ N ☐

Does anyone else know the location? If yes, who? ....

If no one else knows, you should share the location or give an obvious hint.

Location or hint? ....

....

....

LOAN AGREEMENTS

The following are loans that you have given to other people or companies.

To Whom: .... Amount: ....

Contact Information: ....

What are the details of the loan and where is the Promissory Note?

....

To Whom: .... Amount: ....

Contact Information: ....

What are the details of the loan and where is the Promissory Note?

....

To Whom: .... Amount: ....

Contact Information: ....

What are the details of the loan and where is the Promissory Note?

....

ADDITIONAL INFORMATION ABOUT ASSETS

....

....

....

....

....

....

....

....

....

....

....

PERSONAL PROPERTY

This section covers different categories of items, such as jewelry, coins, firearms, artwork, collectibles, etc. We recommend you appraise your items and obtain the proper insurance to cover them in case of loss due to theft, flood, fire, or natural disaster.

Category Name: ....

Have you had any or all items appraised?   Y ☐   N ☐

Do you have an insurance rider on any or all of these items?   Y ☐   N ☐

Have you videotaped or photographed any or all of these items?   Y ☐   N ☐

Where are the photos and/or videos stored? ....

Notes or list of items: ....

....

....

....

....

....

Category Name: ....

Have you had any or all items appraised?   Y ☐   N ☐

Do you have an insurance rider on any or all of these items?   Y ☐   N ☐

Have you videotaped or photographed any or all of these items?   Y ☐   N ☐

Where are the photos and/or videos stored? ....

Notes or list of items: ....

....

....

....

....

....

PERSONAL PROPERTY

Category Name: ....

Have you had any or all items appraised?   Y ☐   N ☐

Do you have an insurance rider on any or all of these items?   Y ☐   N ☐

Have you videotaped or photographed any or all of these items?   Y ☐   N ☐

Where are the photos and/or videos stored? ....

Notes or list of items: ....

....

....

....

....

....

Category Name: ....

Have you had any or all items appraised?   Y ☐   N ☐

Do you have an insurance rider on any or all of these items?   Y ☐   N ☐

Have you videotaped or photographed any or all of these items?   Y ☐   N ☐

Where are the photos and/or videos stored? ....

Notes or list of items: ....

....

....

....

....

....

PERSONAL PROPERTY

Category Name: ....

Have you had any or all items appraised? Y ☐ N ☐

Do you have an insurance rider on any or all of these items? Y ☐ N ☐

Have you videotaped or photographed any or all of these items? Y ☐ N ☐

Where are the photos and/or videos stored? ....

Notes or list of items: ....

....

....

....

....

....

Category Name: ....

Have you had any or all items appraised? Y ☐ N ☐

Do you have an insurance rider on any or all of these items? Y ☐ N ☐

Have you videotaped or photographed any or all of these items? Y ☐ N ☐

Where are the photos and/or videos stored? ....

Notes or list of items: ....

....

....

....

....

MONTHLY BILLS

Company: .... Phone number: ....

Account number: .... Contact name: ....

Bill received by mail or email: ....

What address: ....

How do you pay? .... *Check, Website, Auto-Debit

How often do you pay? .... What amount? *...................

Note: .... *Full, Minimum, Other

Company: .... Phone number: ....

Account number: .... Contact name: ....

Bill received by mail or email: ....

What address: ....

How do you pay? .... *Check, Website, Auto-Debit

How often do you pay? .... What amount? *...................

Note: .... *Full, Minimum, Other

Company: .... Phone number: ....

Account number: .... Contact name: ....

Bill received by mail or email: ....

What address: ....

How do you pay? .... *Check, Website, Auto-Debit

How often do you pay? .... What amount? ....

*Full, Minimum, Other

Company: .... Phone number: ....

Account number: .... Contact name: ....

Bill received by mail or email: ....

What address: ....

How do you pay? .... *Check, Website, Auto-Debit

How often do you pay? .... What amount? *...................

Note: .... *Full, Minimum, Other

Company: .... Phone number: ....

Account number: .... Contact name: ....

Bill received by mail or email: ....

What address: ....

How do you pay? .... *Check, Website, Auto-Debit

How often do you pay? .... What amount? *...................

Note: .... *Full, Minimum, Other

Company: .... Phone number: ....

Account number: .... Contact name: ....

Bill received by mail or email: ....

What address: ....

How do you pay? .... *Check, Website, Auto-Debit

How often do you pay? .... What amount? *...................

Note: .... *Full, Minimum, Other

Company: .... Phone number: ....

Account number: .... Contact name: ....

Bill received by mail or email: ....

What address: ....

How do you pay? .... *Check, Website, Auto-Debit

How often do you pay? .... What amount? *...................

Note: .... *Full, Minimum, Other

Company: .... Phone number: ....

Account number: .... Contact namc: ....

Bill received by mail or email: ....

What address: ....

How do you pay? .... *Check, Website, Auto-Debit

How often do you pay? .... What amount? *...................

Note: .... *Full, Minimum, Other

Company: .... Phone number: ....

Account number: .... Contact name: ....

Bill received by mail or email: ....

What address: ....

How do you pay? .... *Check, Website, Auto-Debit

How often do you pay? .... What amount? *...................

Note: .... *Full, Minimum, Other

Company: .... Phone number: ....

Account number: .... Contact name: ....

Bill received by mail or email: ....

What address: ....

How do you pay? .... *Check, Website, Auto-Debit

How often do you pay? .... What amount? *...................

Note: .... *Full, Minimum, Other

Company: .... Phone number: ....

Account number: .... Contact name: ....

Bill received by mail or email: ....

What address: ....

How do you pay? .... *Check, Website, Auto-Debit

How often do you pay? .... What amount? *...................

Note: .... *Full, Minimum, Other

Company: .... Phone number: ....

Account number: .... Contact name: ....

Bill received by mail or email: ....

What address: ....

How do you pay? .... *Check, Website, Auto-Debit

How often do you pay? .... What amount? *...................

Note: .... *Full, Minimum, Other

SUBSCRIPTIONS, MEMBERSHIPS, AND PUBLICATIONS

Make a list of all your online and hard copy publications, subscriptions, and memberships with dues or payments. You may add login information here or on the Passwords page.

....
....
....
....
....
....
....
....
....
....
....
....
....
....
....
....
....
....
....
....
....
....
....
....
....

HOUSEHOLD INVENTORY

Property Address: ....

Item: .... Room: ....

Description: .... Condition: ....

Purchased where & cost: .... Current value: ....

Model & Serial number: .... Photos or video? Y/N ....

Where are the photos or video? ....

Notes: ....

_____

Item: .... Room: ....

Description: .... Condition: ....

Purchased where & cost: .... Current value: ....

Model & Serial number: .... Photos or video? Y/N ....

Where are the photos or video? ....

Notes: ....

_____

Item: .... Room: ....

Description: .... Condition: ....

Purchased where & cost: .... Current value: ....

Model & Serial number: .... Photos or video? Y/N ....

Where are the photos or video? ....

Notes: ....

_____

Item: .... Room: ....

Description: .... Condition: ....

Purchased where & cost: .... Current value: ....

Model & Serial number: .... Photos or video? Y/N ....

Where are the photos or video? ....

Notes: ....

Item: .... Room: ....

Description: .... Condition: ....

Purchased where & cost: .... Current value: ....

Model & Serial number: .... Photos or video? Y/N ....

Where are the photos or video? ....

Notes: ....

Item: .... Room: ....

Description: .... Condition: ....

Purchased where & cost: .... Current value: ....

Model & Serial number: .... Photos or video? Y/N ....

Where are the photos or video? ....

Notes: ....

Item: .... Room: ....

Description: .... Condition: ....

Purchased where & cost: .... Current value: ....

Model & Serial number: .... Photos or video? Y/N ....

Where are the photos or video? ....

Notes: ....

Item: .... Room: ....

Description: .... Condition: ....

Purchased where & cost: .... Current value: ....

Model & Serial number: .... Photos or video? Y/N ....

Where are the photos or video? ....

Notes: ....

PERSON ONE

ADDITIONAL INFORMATION

PASSWORDS

Name: ....

Company / Site Address	User ID	Password
Cell Phone Password		
Computer Log-in and Password		

PASSWORDS

Name: ....

Company / Site Address	User ID	Password
Cell Phone Password		
Computer Log-in and Password		

MEDICAL INFORMATION

Name: ....Date: ....

Blood Type: .... Height: .... Weight: ....

DOCTORS *(General Practitioner, Dentist, Specialists, Audiology, Internist, Cardiology)*

Doctor: .... Specialty: ....

Phone: ....

Doctor: .... Specialty: ....

Phone: ....

Doctor: .... Specialty: ....

Phone: ....

Doctor: .... Specialty: ....

Phone: ....

Doctor: .... Specialty: ....

Phone: ....

Doctor: .... Specialty: ....

Phone: ....

Veterans Administration Facility: .... Phone: ....

....

DENTAL and VISION

Dentist: .... Phone: ....

Eye Doctor: .... Phone: ....

Where do you buy your contact lenses? ....

Where do you buy your glasses? ....

MEDICAL CONDITIONS

Do you have any medical conditions that require monitoring? ....

....

Do you have any hereditary conditions or risk factors?..

....

MEDICATIONS

Do you take any life sustaining medications? List them here and on your Medications Form

....

....

Are you allergic to any medications? ....

....

MEDICAL EQUIPMENT

Do you use medical equipment? ....

Who is the supplier? .... Phone: ....

Details: ....

....

ALLERGIES

Do you have allergies? List your allergy medications here and on your Medications Form.

....

....

Notes: ....

....

....

VACCINES AND IMMUNIZATIONS

Name: .... Pharmacy: ....

Drug Allergies: ....

Vaccine Name	Date Given	Bundled?	Dosage	Reaction?	Administered by Whom?

MEDICATIONS

Name: ....

Pharmacy: ....

Drug Allergies: ....

Drug Name	Treatment of	Started Taking	Dosage	How Often is the Drug Taken?	Prescribed by Whom?

ESTATE & LEGAL DOCUMENTS

Name: ....

My attorney is: .... Phone: ....

WILL

An attorney is an excellent person to advise you on your Will and ensure that you protect your estate from being overtaxed. In addition, your Will should be kept up-to-date to reflect changes in your family and assets.

Attorney who handled the Will: .... Phone: ....

At the law firm of: ....

Last Will is dated: ....

The executor/executrix is: ....

Are they aware they are the executor? ....

Have you discussed your Will with them? ....

Remind your executor to request multiple copies of your death certificate for accessing your accounts.

Will is stored: .... Copies are stored: ....

ESTABLISHING A TRUST

It may be appropriate to seek your attorney's and financial advisor's advice to determine if establishing a trust fund would benefit your situation.

Title of the Trust: ....

Trustees and contact information: ....

....

....

DURABLE FINANCIAL POWER OF ATTORNEY (POA)

A power of attorney gives someone (your "Agent") the authority to act on your behalf while you are living if you become unable to make decisions for yourself, even for a short period. On your financial POA, you can specify the areas where you want to give power to someone else. Then, upon your death, the executor takes over.

Do you have a Financial POA? .... Effective when? ....

Name of your Agent? ....

Where is your Financial POA stored? ....

NOTES: ....

....

....

LIVING WILL AND HEALTH CARE POWER OF ATTORNEY

A Living Will and Health Care Power of Attorney instruct family members and doctors on what steps you want to be taken should you become unable to make health care decisions for yourself. Distribute originals or copies to your family, doctors, and attorney. Verify that your Living Will specifies that a copy is acceptable.

LIVING WILL OR MEDICAL DIRECTIVE

Do you have a Living Will Declaration?................. Effective when?... ....

To carry out my Living Will, I designate: ....

Have you discussed your wishes with them? ....

The alternate agent is: ....

My Living Will has been given to: ....

Copies are stored: ....

HEALTH CARE POWER OF ATTORNEY (HC POA)

Do you have a Health Care Power of Attorney?: ....

Effective when? ....

As my Health Care POA, I designate: ....

Have you discussed your wishes with them? ....

The alternate agent is: ....

My Health Care Directive has been given to: ....

Copies are stored: ....

ORGAN DONATION

I do ☐   I do not ☐   want any of my organs donated.

I only want the following organs donated: ....

....

NOTES: ....

....

....

IF I'M UNABLE TO COMMUNICATE,

please take care of the following items:

IF I'M UNABLE TO COMMUNICATE,

please take care of the following items:

....

....

....

....

....

....

....

....

....

....

....

....

....

....

....

....

....

....

....

....

....

....

....

FINAL WISHES

DESIGNATIONS

Do you want to designate someone to carry out your wishes for your funeral? Y ☐ N ☐

If yes, who and have you discussed your wishes with them? ....

Do you have money set aside for your funeral? If yes, where? ....

What is your choice for the final disposition of your body?

Burial-traditional in-ground: ....   Burial-above ground: ....

Burial-green: ....   Cremation-traditional: ....

Placement of cremation ashes? ....

....

SERVICE - RELIGIOUS OR MEMORIAL

Type of Service:..

Location: ....

Officiant Name: .... Phone Number: ....

FUNERAL HOME

Funeral Home Preference: ....

Contact Name: .... Phone Number: ....

Have you purchased a package from the funeral home? Y ☐ N ☐

CEMETERY

Cemetery Name: ....

I have a plot in the name of: .... The deed is stored: ....

I am entitled to military honors: Y ☐ N ☐ I am entitled to veterans benefits: Y ☐ N ☐

NOTES: ....

....

....

....

....

VIEWING

If there is a casket, would you like a viewing?

....

Notes: ....

OBITUARY

Would you like to write your Obituary, or is there something you want to be mentioned in your Obituary? If so, write it in the Obituary notes at the end of this section.

SERVICE

Where would you like the service to be held?

....

....

....

....

Please describe the mood or tone of the service you'd like to have.

....

....

....

....

What hymns or music would you like to be played at your service?

....

....

....

....

Which Bible verses, poetry, or readings would you like to be read at your service?

....

....

....

....

SERVICE

Please identify any specific people that you want to be sure are invited to your service.

....

....

....

....

....

....

Who would you like to speak at your service?

....

....

....

....

....

....

Do you have photos or other remembrances that you'd like displayed? Please describe.

....

....

....

....

....

....

Would you like to specify a charity in place of flowers?

....

....

....

....

....

SERVICE

Would you like to give your guests something at the service, such as a program, memorial card, photograph, or bookmark?

....

....

....

....

....

....

MILITARY HONORS

If you are entitled to military honors, would you like to have the flag presentation, and the playing of Taps? Would you like to buried in a VA National Cemetery?

....

....

....

....

....

....

....

....

GRAVESITE

Would you like everyone to be invited to the graveside?

....

....

....

Have you purchased a headstone? If not, what type of headstone would you like to have, and what would you like engraved on it?

....

....

....

....

GRAVESITE

Would you like to specify a special reading?

....

....

....

Is there someone you would like to speak?

....

....

....

Would you like people to place something on your casket?

....

....

RECEPTION OR WAKE

Where would you like the reception or wake to be held?

....

....

....

Who would you like to be invited?

....

....

....

....

....

....

....

....

....

What type of food and refreshments would you like served at the reception?

....

....

POST-RECEPTION ACTIVITY

Would you like your friends and loved ones to do something together or individually to honor you? (Examples: a memorial scholarship, taking a walk, telling stories, etc.)

....

....

....

....

....

ADDTIONAL THOUGHTS AND WISHES

....

....

....

....

....

....

....

....

....

....

....

....

....

....

....

....

....

OBITUARY NOTES

THOUGHTS, WORDS, AND WISHES

THOUGHTS, WORDS, AND WISHES

LETTER TO A LOVED ONE - 1

LETTER TO A LOVED ONE - 1

LETTER TO A LOVED ONE - 2

LETTER TO A LOVED ONE - 2

LETTER TO A LOVED ONE - 3

....
....
....
....
....
....
....
....
....
....
....
....
....
....
....
....
....
....
....
....
....
....
....

LETTER TO A LOVED ONE - 3

MEDICATIONS KEEP THIS PAGE WITH YOU

Name: .... Pharmacy: ....

Drug Allergies: ....

Drug Name	Treatment of	Started Taking	Dosage	How Often is the Drug Taken?	Administered by Whom?

MEDICATIONS

Drug Name	Treatment of	Started Taking	Dosage	How Often is the Drug Taken?	Administered by Whom?

PERSON TWO

ADDITIONAL INFORMATION

ADDITIONAL INFORMATION

PASSWORDS

Name: ....

Company / Site Address	User ID	Password
Cell Phone Password		
Computer Log-in and Password		

PASSWORDS

Name: ....

Company / Site Address	User ID	Password
Cell Phone Password		
Computer Log-in and Password		

MEDICAL INFORMATION

Name: ....Date: ....

Blood Type: .... Height: .... Weight: ....

DOCTORS *(General Practitioner, Dentist, Specialists, Audiology, Internist, Cardiology)*

Doctor: .... Specialty: ....

Phone: ....

Doctor: .... Specialty: ....

Phone: ....

Doctor: .... Specialty: ....

Phone: ....

Doctor: .... Specialty: ....

Phone: ....

Doctor: .... Specialty: ....

Phone: ....

Doctor: .... Specialty: ....

Phone: ....

Veterans Administration Facility: .... Phone: ....

....

DENTAL and VISION

Dentist: .... Phone: ....

Eye Doctor: .... Phone: ....

Where do you buy your contact lenses? ....

Where do you buy your glasses? ....

MEDICAL CONDITIONS

Do you have any medical conditions that require monitoring? ....

....

Do you have any hereditary conditions or risk factors?...................................

....

MEDICATIONS

Do you take any life sustaining medications? List them here and on your Medications Form

....

....

Are you allergic to any medications? ....

....

MEDICAL EQUIPMENT

Do you use medical equipment? ....

Who is the supplier? .... Phone: ....

Details: ....

....

ALLERGIES

Do you have allergies? List your allergy medications here and on your Medications Form.

....

....

Notes: ....

....

....

VACCINES AND IMMUNIZATIONS

Name: .... Pharmacy: ....

Drug Allergies: ....

Vaccine Name	Date Given	Bundled?	Dosage	Reaction?	Administered by Whom?

MEDICATIONS

Name: .... Pharmacy: ....

Drug Allergies: ....

Drug Name	Treatment of	Started Taking	Dosage	How Often is the Drug Taken?	Prescribed by Whom?

ESTATE & LEGAL DOCUMENTS

Name: ....

My attorney is: .... Phone: ....

WILL

An attorney is an excellent person to advise you on your Will and ensure that you protect your estate from being overtaxed. In addition, your Will should be kept up-to-date to reflect changes in your family and assets.

Attorney who handled the Will: .... Phone: ....

At the law firm of: ....

Last Will is dated: ....

The executor/executrix is: ....

Are they aware they are the executor? ....

Have you discussed your Will with them? ....

*Remind your executor to request multiple copies of your death certificate for accessing your accounts.

Will is stored: .... Copies are stored: ....

ESTABLISHING A TRUST

It may be appropriate to seek your attorney's and financial advisor's advice to determine if establishing a trust fund would benefit your situation.

Title of the Trust: ....

Trustees and contact information: ....

....

....

DURABLE FINANCIAL POWER OF ATTORNEY (POA)

A power of attorney gives someone (your "Agent") the authority to act on your behalf while you are living if you become unable to make decisions for yourself, even for a short period. On your financial POA, you can specify the areas where you want to give power to someone else. Then, upon your death, the executor takes over.

Do you have a Financial POA? .... Effective when? ....

Name of your Agent? ....

Where is your Financial POA stored? ....

NOTES: ....

....

....

LIVING WILL AND HEALTH CARE POWER OF ATTORNEY

A Living Will and Health Care Power of Attorney instruct family members and doctors on what steps you want to be taken should you become unable to make health care decisions for yourself. Distribute originals or copies to your family, doctors, and attorney. Verify that your Living Will specifies that a copy is acceptable.

LIVING WILL OR MEDICAL DIRECTIVE

Do you have a Living Will Declaration?................ Effective when?................................

To carry out my Living Will, I designate: ....

Have you discussed your wishes with them? ....

The alternate agent is: ....

My Living Will has been given to: ....

Copies are stored: ....

HEALTH CARE POWER OF ATTORNEY (HC POA)

Do you have a Health Care Power of Attorney?: ....

Effective when? ....

As my Health Care POA, I designate: ....

Have you discussed your wishes with them? ....

The alternate agent is: ....

My Health Care Directive has been given to: ....

Copies are stored: ....

ORGAN DONATION

I do ☐   I do not ☐   want any of my organs donated.

I only want the following organs donated: ....

....

NOTES:...

....

....

IF I'M UNABLE TO COMMUNICATE,

please take care of the following items:

....
....
....
....
....
....
....
....
....
....
....
....
....
....
....
....
....
....
....
....
....
....
....

IF I'M UNABLE TO COMMUNICATE,

please take care of the following items:

....

....

....

....

....

....

....

....

....

....

....

....

....

....

....

....

....

....

....

....

....

....

FINAL WISHES

DESIGNATIONS

Do you want to designate someone to carry out your wishes for your funeral? Y/N

If yes, who and have you discussed your wishes with them? ....

Do you have money set aside for your funeral? If yes, where? ....

What is your choice for the final disposition of your body?

Burial-traditional in-ground: ....   Burial-above ground: ....

Burial-green: ....   Cremation-traditional: ....

Placement of cremation ashes? ....

....

SERVICE - RELIGIOUS OR MEMORIAL

Type of Service:...

Location: ....

Officiant Name: .... Phone Number: ....

FUNERAL HOME

Funeral Home Preference: ....

Contact Name: .... Phone Number: ....

Have you purchased a package from the funeral home? Y ☐   N ☐

CEMETERY

Cemetery Name: ....

I have a plot in the name of: .... The deed is stored: ....

I am entitled to military honors: Y ☐ N ☐   I am entitled to veterans benefits: Y ☐ N ☐

NOTES: ....

....

....

....

....

VIEWING

If there is a casket, would you like a viewing?

....

Notes: ....

OBITUARY

Would you like to write your Obituary, or is there something you want to be mentioned in your Obituary? If so, write it in the Obituary notes at the end of this section.

SERVICE

Where would you like the service to be held?

....

....

....

....

Please describe the mood or tone of the service you'd like to have.

....

....

....

....

What hymns or music would you like to be played at your service?

....

....

....

....

Which Bible verses, poetry, or readings would you like to be read at your service?

....

....

....

....

SERVICE

Please identify any specific people that you want to be sure are invited to your service.

....

....

....

....

....

....

Who would you like to speak at your service?

....

....

....

....

....

Do you have photos or other remembrances that you'd like displayed? Please describe.

....

....

....

....

....

....

Would you like to specify a charity in place of flowers?

....

....

....

....

....

SERVICE

Would you like to give your guests something at the service, such as a program, memorial card, photograph, or bookmark?

....
....
....
....
....
....

MILITARY HONORS

If you are entitled to military honors, would you like to have the flag presentation, and the playing of Taps? Would you like to buried in a VA National Cemetery?

....
....
....
....
....
....
....
....

GRAVESITE

Would you like everyone to be invited to the graveside?

....
....
....

Have you purchased a headstone? If not, what type of headstone would you like to have, and what would you like engraved on it?

....
....
....
....

GRAVESITE

Would you like to specify a special reading?

....

....

....

Is there someone you would like to speak?

....

....

....

Would you like people to place something on your casket?

....

....

RECEPTION OR WAKE

Where would you like the reception or wake to be held?

....

....

....

Who would you like to be invited?

....

....

....

....

....

....

....

What type of food and refreshments would you like served at the reception?

....

....

....

POST-RECEPTION ACTIVITY

Would you like your friends and loved ones to do something together or individually to honor you? (Examples: a memorial scholarship, taking a walk, telling stories, etc.)

....

....

....

....

....

ADDTIONAL THOUGHTS AND WISHES

....

....

....

....

....

....

....

....

....

....

....

....

....

....

....

....

....

....

OBITUARY NOTES

THOUGHTS, WORDS, AND WISHES

THOUGHTS, WORDS, AND WISHES

LETTER TO A LOVED ONE - 1

LETTER TO A LOVED ONE - 1

....

....

....

....

....

....

....

....

....

....

....

....

....

....

....

....

....

....

....

....

....

....

....

LETTER TO A LOVED ONE - 2

LETTER TO A LOVED ONE - 2

....
....
....
....
....
....
....
....
....
....
....
....
....
....
....
....
....
....
....
....
....
....
....
....
....

LETTER TO A LOVED ONE - 3

LETTER TO A LOVED ONE - 3

MEDICATIONS KEEP THIS PAGE WITH YOU

Name: .... Pharmacy: ....

Drug Allergies: ....

Drug Name	Treatment of	Started Taking	Dosage	How Often is the Drug Taken?	Administered by Whom?

MEDICATIONS

Drug Name	Treatment of	Started Taking	Dosage	How Often is the Drug Taken?	Administered by Whom?

Made in the USA
Columbia, SC
23 December 2024

50578808R00067